Just a Moment... of Time...

First published in 2022 by Paragon Publishing, Rothersthorpe
© Ian McGaffney 2022

ISBN 978-1-78222-926-1

Book design, layout and production management by Into Print
www.intoprint.net
+44 (0)1604 832149

Just a moment of time

Ian McGaffney

Just a moment ...

For
Ilyana, Ivan, Christian,
Fabiana, Ian, Ivanova, Sebastian, Maria Corina.

Preface

I have always thought of life as a chain of moments, be
they moments of joy, sadness, loss, hardship, love, success,
disappointment, celebration, family, struggles... I could go on.

Most of the these are real, tangible, attainable - often
emotionally related; some are only fleeting moments, but all
are equal links in an endless, yet curiously, finite chain.

But what about the moments that are not so apparent to
the eye, the moments that take place only in our head,
transformed into words that come together in our mind, and
then overflow onto paper?

The poems presented here are moments; moments of
thought, of feeling, of healing, of dreaming, of smiling,
of time...

"All my possessions for a moment of time."

\- Queen Elizabeth I

of time ...

Just a moment ...

TO THINK

in time…

Senseless

I can see them now,
that violent mob,
the unruly youth,
the gathering storms,
the poor unwashed,
the most uncouth.

You can hear them now,
the silent majority,
the woken mass,
the defenceless forces
against the rising class,
in what results
as a deadly clash.

We can feel them now,
the unpopular measures,
those decisions made,
unable to persuade,
people feeling betrayed,
by destroying all of life's long-lost pleasures.

You can smell them now,
the cans of gas,
the collective scream,
a broken dream,
the tears of pain,
those festering wounds of terror,
that linger and remain.

They sense it now,
the voice unheard,
the rod not spared,
the pain not shared,
as if nobody cared,
about the song of a bird.

in time ...

Now Where?

Nowhere
is a place,
not as far as it seems.
It's somewhere you think of.
Sometimes,
in dreams.

Nowhere
knows no nation,
nor has a banner to show.
A secret location,
that only you know.

Nowhere exists
in the back of your mind.
A place open to visit,
yet others can't find.

Nowhere is fertile,
its seeds can take root.
A hideaway to escape to,
when feelings are moot.

Nowhere
is built out of air.
Made up of thoughts,
and cemented with hope,
a refuge to inhabit,
when unable to cope.

Nowhere
is a state to ponder,
a stage to play,
or act
in your scenes of wonder,
like the endless rainbows
of your wild blue yonder.

in time ...

Just a moment ...

to think

What Rules?

The new rules are there are no more rules.
It now appears that the way to govern
has now been decided
by a witches' coven.

A stubborn spot
which is part of the plot,
brewed and stirred,
into the melting pot.

A recipe for disaster,
but what did it matter,
they thought they were the alternative,
and sent the deniers to scatter.

No regard for the past,
they were sure this was the future,
and thought that the world could be healed
with just a small suture.

The burning and looting,
was just an excuse for the masses.
In the wake of a shooting,
rose the ire of the classes.

How delusional they would seem,
making no sense with their acts.
Following an impossible dream,
without considering the facts.

in time ...

Just a moment …

to think

The Past is the Past

Why won't the masses let history be?
Stop them trying to rewrite the past
whilst tumbling erstwhile heroes,
or make us bend at the knee.

Let those stony reminders
stand tall in their moment,
silently telling us,
it was their sole destiny.

in time ...

Just a moment …

to think

Disunited States

A young and proud state,
once the home of the brave and the free,
now consumed by evil and hate,
and forced to bend at the knee.

The assault on the hill,
in such an unruly, violent manner,
shouting the right to bear arms,
linked together with brothers,
inflicting senseless harm
on so many others.
Now everybody's facing a bill,
for burning a star-mangled banner.

in time ...

Just a moment ...

to think

The Red Planet

It's a slow drip
that erodes old values,
drowns all of your dreams,
stifles the thoughts,
and pulls lives apart at the seams.

Shrouded in darkness,
always working in shade,
imposing a mindset,
and ways to behave.
Promising justice for all,
but only administering misery
from cradle to grave.

Promising everything equal
yet nothing, nor anybody,
remaining the same.

Driving the world to the edge
people would reach for the stars.
As a matter of survival,
we preferred to travel to Mars.

in time ...

Just a moment ...

to think

Animal Instinct

If the truth were to be told,
if politicians became bold,
instead of to scold,
we'd come back to the fold,
come in from the cold,
and enjoy growing old.

No matter how low they stoop,
they'd continue to dupe.
Keep others out of the loop,
and never recoup,
the chicks back in the coop,
instead of ending in soup.

They've never been able
to put their cards on the table
They just keep telling the fable,
and keep the horses in stable.

in time ...

Just a moment ...

to think

Why on Earth?

Why on earth
the people
don't stop to think,
that their selfish ways,
are condemning all of mankind
to a life on the brink?

When on earth
will the people
eventually learn,
that they must change their deeds
before their time doth come,
and the tide starts to turn?

Who on earth ever thought,
that the same old people
would be blind to the signs,
and deaf to the calls,
about the havoc they wrought?

What on earth
made the people behave like this,
to pursue self-destruction,
with no looking back
from the edge of the abyss?

Where on earth,
before it's too late,
will those like-minded souls,
take control of the future,
and change the course of our fate?

in time …

Just a moment ...

to think

Escalation – by The Book

Rival factions
Covert actions
Insinuations
Allegations
Provocations
Aggravations
Implications
Overreaction
Imposing sanctions
Gaining traction
Strained relations
Battle stations
Warring nations
Nuclear reactions
Conflagration
Devastation
Annihilation
Congregation
God's creation
Revelation

in time ...

Just a moment ...

to think

Going Nuclear

They would all start a new race,
and we could see what they muster,
whilst they pick up the pace
as a result of the bluster.

At the end of the day
it was a matter of fate,
there remained only one way,
and nobody could wait.

They were playing with fire.
and thought they should do what they must.
It was nobody's desire,
to turn us all into dust.

Yet the world couldn't wait to get started
to see how it would end.
Now we all have departed,
there are no more bridges to mend.

in time ...

Just a moment ...

to think

Watch this Space!

We could lie down side by side,
to visit the moon in all its glory,
await a turn in the eventual tide,
and begin a journey that ends in a story.

We could float amongst the firmament's stars,
and bathe in their brilliant light.
Search the sky for one without scars,
never letting them out of our sight.

We'd reach out desperately for a friend on Mars,
whilst looking down on the sorry states,
knowing that they were no longer ours,
after having destroyed all that dear God creates.

in time ...

Just a moment ...

to think

Written in Stone

Words are often written in stone.
They should be formed, sculpted,
and each given a meaning.
A solid foundation on which to rest their letters.

Eventually eroded by time and opinions
that rub against their grain,
creating distortions and fissures,
then dissolved with the rain.

Words should never be written in stone.
Only those in the memory of the dearly departed,
and for our beloved ones, long since gone.

in time ...

Just a moment ...

to think

Down to Earth

Return to earth,
heaven can wait.
Let's get back to basics,
before it's too late.

Time to reset
the famed doomsday clock,
and stop just listening
to that relentless tick-tock.

The ice caps are melting
and the tides are turning.
We can't just stand by
whilst the fires keep on burning.

There must be a way
to end all of this madness.
On us it depends
if we plunge the world into sadness.

in time …

Just a moment …

TO FEEL

some time …

Just a moment ...

to feel

Moonrise

That perfect brilliant moon,
rising slowly into a starless night,
sending slivers of silver,
like extending fingers
over a silent sea.

They reach out to the shore,
barely shifting the sand.
Just a caressing hand,
that reached out to me.

some time ...

Solitude, or is it Just Me?

"I"
A lonely letter.
Somewhat like me.
I enjoy my solitude,
the peace, the quiet,
the tranquillity.

Yes, it's a lonely place,
where you can hear your thoughts,
even your body speaking to you.
You can dream your dreams,
of whatever pleasures sought.

No interruptions
make your mind more aware,
of the slightest movement,
or of the minutes passing,
with never a care.

Solitude is freedom.
It is listening to music or opening a book,
or walking in the park,
crossing a path,
without having to look.

That lonely letter
should never complain,
but live and enjoy every moment,
of the company of others,
whilst the feelings remain.

I
like being alone,
but am never lonely.
I have my thoughts,
words to accompany me,
and to remind me that I am not the only
one.

some time ...

A Place to Hide

It's dark,
it's cold,
and here I am.
Alone again,
and I'm lonely,
here within the confines of my four walls
that are the outer layers of my skin.

I have an adjacent room that is my mind.
It is here to where I go, by-passing my heart,
and where I will spend most of my time.

I am surprised at the size of this room.
The amount of storage space is unbelievable.
The corridors, the open areas. Really amazing!
I have so much stuff in here, I sometimes misplace it
or can't find certain things.
At times they just don't come to mind.

It is a wonderful place to stay.
A place that changes every day depending on many factors,
but mainly due to what enters through the two windows that
look out on my day - or night for that matter.
It is not a place like the heart
which just goes pump-pump-pump all day long,
barely missing a beat.
Boring. Or is it? After all, that's where love lives.

I can spend hours in here doing repetitive tasks,
going over them again and again, trying to perfect them.
They don't always end up right.
It could go on forever.
I might just pack them away and use them later.
Funny, I hardly feel tired when I'm in this room, even though
there is so much to do to keep me occupied.

I often meet with angels, and there are always plenty
of demons visiting.
Many of them are permanent residents.
There is just so much room here for both of them.
The discussions between these two can be really heated.
It is an ongoing battle.

I also have some inconsiderate neighbours.
They are constantly making a noise.
I have to bang on their walls now and then, but
they don't hear me or don't want to listen.
I try to ignore them, and I suppose I will eventually become
used to them. Still, they can be a pain now and then.

I sometimes wish I could get out more. Maybe visit new
places or see other people.

I wonder if I am trapped.

Could I escape?

Maybe I am already free.

some time …

Upon Reflection

A series of mirrors
will follow you through life,
regular reminders
of pleasure or of strife.
They reflect on your image,
and help you on decisions to change.
Telling you silently
there are several parts to arrange.

Don't be afraid to stare
into the dark rings of your eyes.
It is said they are the path that leads to your soul,
so why would you think
that they look back so old?

The changes you see,
as time passes you by,
tell your life story,
seen by more than one's eyes.

There's no altering the truth,
that we all are obliged to face.
Everything is apparent,
as to how the changes took place

They won't help you see the future,
but just reflect on your past.
You would be naive to even think
that it ever could last.
What you thought was an illusion,
is just another part of your delusion.

some time …

Just a moment …

to feel

.

Life Making Sense

Find a taste
for all that is good.
The drink and the food.
Enjoy your job,
your livelihood.

Educate your nose,
Discover a scent.
An envelope sent,
a secret love,
a passion to vent.

Develop a touch.
Embrace a feel.
A moment to steal
a warm embrace,
a meaning so real.

Open your eyes,
broaden your sight.
Board a ship in the night
blinded to what's right,
whilst holding her tight.

Listen to your heart,
hear all that's been said.
Forget all the dread,
live your own life,
clear out your head.

some time ...

Just a moment …

to feel

Life Time

Time has its limits,
they say it waits for no man.
So, not a minute to be wasted,
make the most of it whilst you can.

Time has no limits,
so, make a break with the past.
Live your dreams to the fullest.
Forever does not last.

Time has its limits,
it's part of daily life.
Breathe every moment you are given,
accept the inward strife.

Time has its limits,
it watches your whole life unfold.
That clock you hear ticking,
is just your heart growing old.

Time has its limits,
it takes its toll every day,
measures every second that passes,
before passing away.

some time ...

Just a moment …

to feel

Prisoner

You build and enter your own dungeon,
barely able to see.
You lock yourself in,
misplacing the key.

Nobody to blame,
it's only your fault.
Maybe it's a shame
that you're trapped in a vault.

You waited and waited
until almost too late,
hoping somebody else
would decide on your fate.

You had time on your hands
to ponder your pride.
But it disappeared in the sand,
washed away by the tide.

All that remains
is a sorrowful soul,
devoid of all feeling,
and with a heart growing old.

some time ...

Just a moment ...

to feel

Where does Love go?

Where does love go?
Does it disappear into increasingly rare air,
suffocating those gasping last minutes,
as if nobody ever did care?

Love is the fire that burns bright through the night,
always there right from the start,
binding two little words before God,
promising until death do us part.
In truth, it stays only as long as you want,
until ready to take leave of your heart.

Without love the fire might start to wane,
the flame could diminish and die,
often too late to rekindle the ashes,
with everyone wondering why.

Over years love was replaced with just pain,
in time it just wanted no more.
It knew things could never be the same,
and love would finally walk out the door.

some time ...

Just a moment …

to feel

(P) Ending

The wheels kept turning,
but there was no more earning,
yet the mind was learning
as the body stopped caring,
and the stomach was churning
when the heart stopped burning.
It was most concerning
that there was no more yearning.

some time ...

Just a moment ...

to feel

Cowered

I should have walked into the war,
and fought my battles from the front,
instead of lying in the trenches,
watching my bayonet become blunt.

I could have decided not to wait,
and gone in over the top.
Begin a confrontation,
start a movement that wouldn't stop.

I could have taken that decision
instead of lamenting whilst I await.
Or start to move ahead with such precision,
but now it's just too late.

The lack of courage has a price,
it never compensates for such a loss.
Regretting will never suffice,
and now I am forever to carry this cross.

some time ...

Just a moment ...

to feel

Delays

So why do you wait
until it's too late?
Is it so hard to relate,
whilst avoiding your fate?

It is what it is,
face up to the fact.
There are no excuses,
for the courage you lacked.

You might have enacted,
played up to your heart,
remembered the lines,
that tore you apart.

Maybe the fire has burnt out,
or your feelings are in retreat,
replaced with a coldness,
where once a heart truly beat.

some time …

Just a moment …

to feel

No Way Back

You can't go back
it just won't be right.
Doing things
that only hurt yourself,
will keep you awake late at night.

It's not good for your body,
your mind or your soul.
It never ends well,
if the truth would be told.

You must take back the control.
It's only your decision.
Didn't you understand?
Didn't you see the vision?

You better make haste,
your time will run out.
There's not a moment to waste,
it's what life's all about.

some time …

Just a moment ...

to feel

The Bird

I found her by the wayside,
a bird with a broken wing.
A face scared and full of pain,
and a voice that could barely sing.

I held her gently, cupped in my hands,
felt the trembling deep in the heart.
I saw the eyes pleading for help,
and knew I could never depart.

I cared and fed her for weeks on end,
sensed the strength returning day by day.
I saw how her wing started to mend,
and I knew that soon she would be on her way.

The bird would accompany me wherever I went,
eating out of my hand whilst all could see.
The light in her eyes, and the message they sent:
she knew that one day she'd want to be free.

some time ...

Just a moment ...

to feel

Calm

Let me hold you close to my heart,
wipe away all your tears,
bring life into your dreams,
put aside all those fears.

Let me take your warm hand,
on a long summer's day.
Let's take a walk in the sand,
I'll show you the way.

Let me give you your calm,
whisper loving words in your ear.
Hold you in a never-ending embrace,
and show you all that is dear.

Let us wake up and fly,
reach out for the stars,
the sun and the moon.
Travelling afar,
not a moment too soon.

some time …

Just a moment ...

to feel

The Circus

Does your mind ever wander,
wonder about life,
as if walking through circuses,
balancing acts, performing incredible feats,
on the edge of a knife.

The ringmaster enters,
in control as announces,
the crowd gasps for air,
as the animal pounces.

The acrobat soars,
without making a slip,
afraid to look down,
in case he loses his grip.

The clown plays to the crowd,
painted smile just a mask.
Hiding pain and the sorrow,
not up to the task.
Yet knowing all well
that the show must go on,
come heaven or hell,
with no thought of tomorrow.

some time ...

Just a moment ...

to feel

Feelings

I should dig deeper
I know they are in there somewhere.
I should have tried harder.
I'm certain I'll find them.
I'm sure I put them in my pocket full of dreams before I went
to bed.
Maybe I took them out before sleeping?
Or even lost the desire before dropping off?
It is possible they got caught on my sleeve as I rummaged
around in my pockets.
Or they fell onto the floor and got kicked under the door
without my knowing or realising what happened.

I wonder if I will ever find them again.
If I do, I will make sure I keep them in a safe place and use
them sparingly.
They shouldn't be wasted and certainly not at this time of life.

It would be a shame if I lost them forever.
I already miss them in a way.
Yet I should not dwell.
I just hope they turn up somewhere, or somebody else finds
them and returns them to me.
Anyway, time alone will tell.

some time …

Just a moment ...

to feel

Sunset

There is something magic
about watching the setting sun
melt into a tranquil sea on a distant horizon,
from an autumn shore.

There is a certain peace
in the painted skies, the subtle hues,
the fading light of nature's goodbyes,
that leave you in awe.

some time ...

Just a moment ...

TO HEAL

with time ...

Just a moment ...

to heal

Just Maybe

Maybe I visit you again.
Just walk in,
unannounced,
as I sometimes do.
Maybe I knock on your door,
or give you a call in advance.
I might even wake you up,
give you a chance
to gather your thoughts.
You probably imagined,
or maybe you felt sure,
that you would never see me again.
But you know me,
I like to catch people by surprise.
Most people don't like that.
They like to get themselves ready,
or maybe they prefer not to answer the door,
or don't want to see me again.
People can be so sensitive,
or even take me too seriously.
Maybe they just don't want me to get to know them,
or see how they are, show how they really are.
Probably they just want to ignore me and hope I go away.
Anyway, I know when I'm not welcome.
Maybe I go and visit somebody else.
It just may be.

with time …

Just a moment ...

to heal

Cancer in the building

You could remove all the doors,
maybe tear down the walls,
take away all that was yours
whilst the roof finally falls.

Love might linger a while,
where once there was trust,
yet, with such a difference in style,
it all turned into dust.

You would cause nothing but trouble
as you destroyed all the good in the cells,
watching them turn into rubble,
as the damage just continued to swell.

Then arrived a new foundation,
you were forced by hand to rebuild.
The workers would try to evict you,
from where before you had killed.

with time …

Just a moment …

to heal

A Dark Place

You will stare into the chasm,
an endless abyss.
Fearful of the images presented,
or of what went amiss.

You look deeper and deeper
into the eyes without hope,
reflecting the future
where unable to cope.

Don't be afraid of the dark,
you won't be alone.
There will be someone to guide you,
and lead you back to your home.

with time …

Just a moment ...

to heal

Damocles

That sword you wield with silent ease,
hovering above me, holding my life to ransom
whenever you deem to please.
Your presence emerges every quarter,
awaiting a sign, or a moment to strike,
taking advantage of a chink in my shield.
With a swipe of the blade
you erase parts of my life,
hoping that I will eventually yield.

with time ...

Just a moment ...

to heal

You Again...

I will find you
in my dreams,
somewhere.
I know you are there.
Waiting.
Hesitating.
Why should I care?

I have to accept,
there are always clouds in the sky.
If life was so easy
we'd be going our way,
and stop even thinking,
why you wanted to stay.

Just looking around me,
searching for a simple way out,
but you're there right beside me,
silent,
with never a doubt.

with time ...

Just a moment ...

to heal

Dear Cancer,

I thought I was over you.
I mean, it's been long enough.
I've been thinking of you now and then.
Although I must admit, sometimes I just can't get you out of
my mind.

I thought you might have been ringing me.
That's what I'd heard anyway.
I know you still have my number.

You know, I often wondered
what it would be like to live life without you.
I would probably never be the same.
You'd always leave an impression on me; not always good!

By the way, you left some things with me.
Did you do that on purpose to remind me of you?
Maybe you want to drop in sometime.
You might even want to hang around for a while,
or even move back with me forever.
Who knows...relationships can be difficult sometimes, but
maybe we can come to an arrangement.
Maybe you want to take the rest of your things and leave me
with nothing...
or is it that you want to move in permanently?
I don't think that's a good idea.
It never ends well...

with time ...

Just a moment ...

to heal

Feeling Odd, Even Up

I have a feeling,
and it's not going away.
I don't want to think about it,
but it's probably here to stay.

It knows about time,
and how it waits
for no man.
It will wreak its damage,
however it can.

You can feel by touch,
convince yourself it's not much,
but you know it is there,
and it just doesn't care

You will wait and await,
maybe sometimes too late.
It might even be better
just accepting your fate.

You're here to take back,
what you think is all yours.
You think you have earned it,
and you will level the course.

with time …

Just a moment ...

to heal

The Witching Hour

The witching hour
casts its spell,
on thoughts and words,
only mine to tell,
all about suffering
a private hell.
Burning within,
yet unable to quell,
the flames that consume me,
as the death bells knell.

with time ...

Just a moment …

to heal

Faith

Yes, you need something,
someone,
to show you the way.
A leading light,
to a path in the night,
that helps as you pray.

You will eventually find,
someone equally kind,
if only to soothe
your anger
that invades you,
and never leaves you,
with nothing to choose.

You've agreed with your maker,
made your peace with your friends.
Met with your forsaker,
and made all your amends.

with time …

Just a moment ...

to heal

Appealing to Faith

Those distant bells
are calling those who choose
to show their faith
in a different place
when they've nothing to lose.

Those distant bells
are for those afar and near,
to guide them to peace,
a final release,
with nothing to fear.

Those distant bells
are ringing loud and true.
A constant reminder
that there is somewhere much kinder,
which is waiting for you.

Those distant bells
remain year after year.
A leading light
in a cold, dark night,
to those willing to hear.

Those distant bells,
with their melancholy knell,
are showing the way,
to those deciding to stay,
and face their own private hell.

with time …

Just a moment …

to heal

The Wishing Well

Many people would visit,
greet with many a kind word.
They made their request,
said all of their prayers,
and hoped for the best.

They tried to understand,
but all is not what it seems.
A drop in the darkness,
impossible to fill,
an empty bucket of dreams.

Hope drowned in the depths,
tears welling in circles,
falling like rain.
Giving their best to their wishes
with the pennies from heaven,
and I'm so glad that they came.

with time ...

Just a moment ...

to heal

Feeling Cancer

I could peel the words from the walls,
wipe the tears off the floor,
put the pain in my pocket,
and crawl out the door.

I would feel your disease
as it grew in my neck.
Think nothing was happening,
whilst I turned into a wreck.

I barely noticed your presence,
yet the signs were all there.
You had no intention of leaving,
and what did you care.

I would lay down with you
in the dark of the night.
I could sense your ill feeling
and faced up to my plight.

with time …

Just a moment ...

to heal

On Return

I knew you would return,
I could feel you were coming.
You can't leave me alone,
yet you think I will welcome you,
as if this were your home.

There's no way you are staying,
I'll hide under the stares,
go on forever delaying,
and start reciting my prayers.

Stop all your intentions,
they are always something to fear.
You still don't understand,
I never want you this near.

Do you really think it would be fair?
That you should share my life,
pretending you care,
as if you were my wife!

You might tell me you still love me,
but your words aren't sincere,
I've told you before:
you no longer live here!

with time ...

Just a moment ...

TO DREAM

any time …

So...What?

There's a door.
It's ajar.
I could walk through it.
But I don't.
Instead,
I close it.

There's a window.
It's broken.
Cracked, shattered.
I look out.
My view is distorted.

There is a road.
It is a way out of here.
Maybe.
It's strewn with rubble.
Or is it broken glass?
Anyway,
I am barefooted.

There's a bed.
It's empty,
and it's cold.
I lie down,
but I don't sleep.

There's a sea of dreams.
I see angels.
Or are they demons?
I am floating.
Or am I sinking?

of time …

Just a moment …

to dream

Always in Dreams

You could spend your whole life
chasing your shadows,
running towards them,
or running away.
Following the rainbows.
searching for gold.
Living your dreams
before you get old.

Or gaze at the night sky,
counting the stars,
shooting in a darkness
that envelopes your soul.
Falling in space
with nothing to hold.
Your arms outstretched,
not even feeling the cold.

You might grasp at the moon,
clutch some dust in your hands,
spreading the sparkle
as you look where it lands.
Arriving on earth
to see where it starts.
Keep your eyes on the road,
and follow your heart.

of time …

Just a moment …

to dream

Chasing Clouds

I closed my eyes,
and laid my head on the pillow,
chasing the clouds
as they started to billow.

I was pursuing my dreams,
in search of clear skies,
preferring the purest of truth,
to a nightmare of lies.

The plumes would escape me,
constantly changing their forms,
leaving me grasping at nothing,
whilst announcing the storms.

The clouds would weigh heavy,
as the skies became overcast.
The rain washed away all my dreams,
whilst drowning the past...

of time ...

Just a moment ...

to dream

The Night Time

The eyes remain closed.
It is darker than you thought.
Hiding from view the exposed images,
of the battles you have fought.

It is deeper than you think,
it takes time to take its toll.
The drying of the ink
is just a reflection of the soul.

Don't waste time on empty thoughts,
that poison good words often found.
Take heed of those you only sought,
cherish, and remember, their soft, loving sound.

of time ...

Just a moment ...

to dream

Mind Games

Have you ever wondered
how it would be
to wander and find,
the myriad corridors,
the endless maze,
of an open mind.

Visiting cluttered rooms,
some empty cells,
yet searching for answers
from those silent people
who never would tell.

You look for solutions,
amid the cogs slowly turning.
Part of a quiet revolution,
whilst the fires kept on burning.

You never reach a conclusion,
an end to the game.
Just another illusion,
maybe even a delusion,
as everything, always,
remains just the same.

of time ...

Just a moment …

to dream

A Walk in the Park

I shuffled through the deserted park,
my only witnesses the empty benches
forming sinister shapes in the approaching dark.
Who knows what confessions they might have heard
from disillusioned lovers, secret trysts, sisters, and brothers.

Those long, lonely walks.
The autumn breeze rolling in under an overcast sky.
Untethered leaves
floating and fleeting, swirling and curling,
ending their journey trampled underfoot,
like the endless ramblings of our intimate talks.

Alone with my thoughts,
ambitious in stature,
carved out of dreams long since passed.
Falling into step whilst I become oblivious to my distorted
shadow
that overtakes me.
Leaving me chasing after all that is sought.

of time ...

Just a moment …

to dream

The Song of the Lark

A walk in the park
A passing glance
A distant bark
The song of a lark

A meeting by chance
A kiss in the dark
A very slow dance
The start of romance

The seductive smiles
A difference in styles
A move that beguiles
A deed that defiles

A look in the eyes
The lows and the highs
The murmurs and sighs
A flash of the thighs
A pleasant surprise

A beautiful lass
A lay in the grass
A feeling so crass
All things must pass

The thoughts in the head
The mind being read
The words left unsaid
A feeling of dread
A love that was dead

of time …

Just a moment ...

to dream

Seasons

I carry you with me,
you are no burden to bear.
I feel your breath, a cool mist that greets me,
in the cold winter's air.

I carry you with me,
every step of the way.
Rustling the autumn leaves,
following each golden sunset,
at the end of the day.

I carry you with me,
I promised I'd be there,
whilst the summers warm breeze
sways the strands of your hair.

I carry you with me,
in every beat of the heart.
The spring heralds a new beginning,
a new life to start.

of time …

Just a moment …

to dream

0340

I'd lie there.
Staring hard at the shifting shapes
partially illuminated by slivers of light,
peering in through cracks in the hotel's curtains.
Yes, I'd just lie there trying to recall those crazy scenes
alive in my head.

I'd close my eyes
and fall consciously into a rabbit hole that led to my
Wonderland.
Deeper and darker I would fall, searching for that sleep fairy.
A maze that led nowhere.
Yes, I'd just lie there,
drifting in and out of my dreams,
but still awake in my bed.

of time ...

Just a moment …

to dream

Heaven or Hell

Whilst you might lay still,
oft against your will,
you close your eyes
and see an endless space,
darker than a starless night.

You'll drift down to the depths
or float up to the sky,
searching for answers
and wondering why
you never could find
a light that would guide you
as you left reason behind.

of time …

Just a moment ...

to dream

Sometimes, However...

Sometimes,
in my dreams,
I would build castles in the sky.
Soaring towers,
reaching high.

However,
the towers would crumble,
things would not work out as planned.
I soon realised
that their very foundations
were made out of sand.

of time ...

Just a moment ...

to dream

Heart

I know you are with me always.
I feel your warmth when next to me.
You flutter when I suffer,
yet never miss a beat.

You share my pain regardless,
even when the rest of me falls apart.
You are my very reason for living.
After all, you are my heart.

of time ...

Human...being

I go to sleep.
But I don't.
Maybe I float, or drift,
off into the night
like a small craft breaking free of its moorings,
on a calm, silent sea.
I might howl at the moon,
fight my demons until dawn.
They just won't let me be,
leaving me broken and forlorn.

I dream.
Sometimes
I can see you all,
past and present.
I might pass you on corners.
Only a fleeting glance
of silver hair.
But never the faces,
sometimes not even the places.
Yes, we are all growing old.
Maybe too old to care.

I wake.
Maybe I'll walk.
And I talk.
Sometimes to others,
but mainly to myself.
I am a better listener
after all.
I'll ask myself questions,
what life's all about.
Not having the answers,
but attending the call.

I pray.
I am alone.
In the company of strangers,
just kneeling or lying there.
As time passes by
I will join them in prayers,
cry their tears and share their laughter.
I shall rest in my peace, in the silence,
and remain with them thereafter.

of time ...

Just a moment ...

TO SMILE

of time ...

Becoming of Age

Against all the odds,
and with barely a scar,
all bets are now off
after you made it this far.

You awake in the morning
to the aches and the pain.
Take it easy upon rising
in case of a strain.

What once was a chill
turns into a full blown cold.
Taking longer to recover
means you're just getting old.

Crumbling and creaking,
your knees need repair.
The gaps in your mouth now need filling,
and your skin needs more care.

The hair at your temples
are all shades of grey.
On their way to turn white,
before fading away.

The bald spot starts showing,
you are thinning on top.
A toupee's insufficient,
you need to plug it to stop!

Your hearing is impaired,
the ringing starts in your ears.
They are just further signs
of your advancing in years.

The wrinkles and crinkles
take control of your face.
When you look in the mirror
they're all over the place!

The shrinkage has started,
not always in sight.
And sorry to say,
it's not all about height.

The soft shoe shuffle
has turned into your gait.
Sooner or later,
the wheelchair awaits.

Your eyes grow weaker,
and the light seems much dimmer.
Your balance becomes shaky,
as you reach out for your Zimmer.

Soon in the twilight,
the mind is starting to roam.
Then all of a sudden,
there's a new meaning for home.

any time …

Just a moment ...

to smile

Seventy

So, what happens now?
You've reached three score and ten.
It is written to end here,
for all women and men.

The aches and the pains
are par for the course.
Don't give up the game,
forget all the remorse.

How long does it take
for the body to break?
Better start making plans,
before it's too late.

Try to steal some more years,
there's time later for rest.
If you get to have more,
then you really are blessed.

It's just one part of life,
so, accept it's your fate.
Prepare for the waiting
at God's Golden Gate.

Face up to your truth,
It's a kind of release.
Leave everything behind,
and just Rest in Peace.

any time ...

Just a moment ...

to smile

A Body Driven

Don't take your eyes off the road,
not even a blink.
There's too much to see.
So, seek out your way,
keep your mind focused,
and live for the day.

Face up to the future,
and walk tall as you move,
keeping pace with your journey.
Stick your neck out, if need be,
take the bends in your stride.
Bow your head if you must:
you've got nothing to hide.

Keep your fears at arm's length,
and your dreams within reach.
Don't point fingers at others,
but offer your hand.
Feel grateful for blessings,
and strive to understand.

Get your foot in the door,
accept a leg up.
Yet work shoulder to shoulder,
and don't let your heart ever crack.
The more you go farther,
there's no turning back.

any time ...

Just a moment ...

to smile

Growing Pains

It all went by
in the blink of an eye.
Yet from the primal scream,
to the first wet dream,
the days went slow
until given the go.

The days seemed longer
whilst our bodies grew stronger.
The innocence of youth
disappeared with the truth.

The change in the voices
meant we started to make choices.
Fuelled by friends and some learning,
our future would start to take shape
whilst the wheels kept on turning.

A stolen first kiss
from an all too willing Miss
felt like heavenly bliss.
Then we soon realised
the full meaning of sighs.

We'd run with the crowd
whilst shouting out loud,
not stopping to ask ourselves why,
as our life passed us by.

any time ...

Just a moment …

to smile

Old News

There were times when the telegraph would be quicker than the post, but not as fast as today's mail.

The reporter would use a runner who would eventually become an enquirer.

A keen observer, or even a spectator, would see the sun reflect in the mirror,

and have the express need to record or echo events and chronicle them in a sketch of interest to the people.

Just for the record, this would be news of the world and travel around the globe.

They play the last post on the bugle and would lower the standard in the evening, and it would end up just like a rag.

any time …

Just a moment ...

to smile

Ethereal

Such a heavenly body.
Just out of this world.
An angel sent from heaven.
What a hell of a girl!

any time...

Just a moment ...

Acknowledgements

Special thanks to Anne and Mark at Into Print, particularly to Anne for her insight, input, creativity, and her patience in putting the book together.

Thanks also to Ana Maria for her usual support from afar!

Finally, my thanks to all those who gave me *Just a Moment... of Time.*

About the Author

Ian was born on December 17th, 1951, in Liverpool, UK, and emigrated to South America in 1974, where he lived for over 40 years. He is retired and has been living in Madrid since 2016. He has three children and five grandchildren.

His first book *Dear Cancer, With love...* was published in 2020, followed by *Life, and so on...* later the same year.

In 2021 his first book in Spanish, *Pensamientos...en otras palabras...* was published.

Just a Moment... of Time, is a reflection on past and present times.

any time ...

www.ingramcontent.com/pod-product-compliance
Lightning Source LLC
LaVergne TN
LVHW041156080426
835511LV00006B/630